Jasmine

Your fragrance lingers…

A psychotherapist's personal account of her journey of grief

(Integrating Science, Philosophy, and the story of Creation)

Rachel Bates

notionpress.com

INDIA · SINGAPORE · MALAYSIA

Copyright © Rachel Bates 2022
All Rights Reserved.

ISBN 979-8-88749-884-3

This book has been published with all efforts taken to make the material error-free after the consent of the author. However, the author and the publisher do not assume and hereby disclaim any liability to any party for any loss, damage, or disruption caused by errors or omissions, whether such errors or omissions result from negligence, accident, or any other cause.

While every effort has been made to avoid any mistake or omission, this publication is being sold on the condition and understanding that neither the author nor the publishers or printers would be liable in any manner to any person by reason of any mistake or omission in this publication or for any action taken or omitted to be taken or advice rendered or accepted on the basis of this work. For any defect in printing or binding the publishers will be liable only to replace the defective copy by another copy of this work then available.

Jasmine: Gift from God

CONTENTS

Foreword vii
Reviews ix
Preface xiii
Dedication xvii
Acknowledgements xix
Prologue xxi

1. Crushed, but not Defeated 1
2. Darkness can Produce Light 16
3. Pain can Disable or Enable 20
4. Joy is a Given, Happiness is a Choice 25
5. A Mother's Love: What it can do 35
6. Love Activates Joy; Joy Produces Happiness 52
7. Finding Meaning in Grief 59
8. Grief at its Best ... 71
9. Tears: Is it ok to Cry? 83
10. Is Death the End of Existence? 91

Epilogue 105

FOREWORD

I became acquainted with Rachel Bates, in her professional capacity, several months ago. I was in a state of bewilderment, guilt, and grief, all of my own. Rachel offered an oasis of calm, faith-filled thoughtfulness and gentle wisdom that pulled me through the most profound depths of my crisis.

A heart-on-the-sleeve author, myself, I have appreciated the raw honesty of this book, 'Jasmine - your fragrance lingers' and its account, almost in real-time, of a personal journey through the process of deep grieving. Yet this short book is so much more than that. Drawing upon Rachel's wealth of professional experience and core-deep faith in the Living God, this journey reaches out to the reader, offering tools and understanding that minister to the reader and facilitate healthy ways of embracing the stages of grief.

Rachel's appreciation, love, and even adoration of her mother Jasmine is emphatically expressed with great vulnerability throughout the book. However, the force of these powerful emotions is then examined and harnessed into valuable professional insights and analysis, to make clear to the reader, the eternal perspective of life and death, and to offer real, tangible hope in place of despair.

Open your heart, your very spirit, as you read this book and it will minister to you and prepare you, in a most beautiful, articulate way, for the inevitability of facing those most profound and inescapable realities of both this existence and the existence still to come. Could we, too, leave a beautiful lingering fragrance, for the generations to come?

Simon Day
Author of:
A Tale of Two CVS

REVIEWS

"This book is a Godsend. It is a powerful insight and articulation of the journey of personal loss and tragedy. Rachel approaches her own journey of grief with vulnerability and candour. This resource is useful for both people who need to find their own voice for handling personal loss, and for those who will take the time to listen and who desire to reach out to the broken-hearted. As you read this book, your own eyes will be opened, your heart challenged, and your resolve strengthened to be God's hands and feet to a hurting world".

- **Rev. Dave Taylor, pastor of Elim Family Church, Southwater, UK**

"Jasmine, your fragrance lingers, is the journey of bereavement written in total honesty and openness. This is not analysed material; it is a real person expressing real pain in a real way. Using her own sorrow and pain, Rachel demonstrates how one can navigate their journey of grief. I would recommend this book to everyone, as grief is part of life, but specifically, to those who have lost a loved one".

- **Rev. David Eaton, Elder at New Life Church, Crawley, UK**

"In writing a very touching, heartfelt and a loving tribute to her mother Jasmine, Rachel articulates her own personal journey through loss, darkness, grieving and finally letting go, through her professional understanding of grief and the process of grieving. Rachel intersperses the chapters seamlessly with her professional expertise. This is a wonderful tribute to an extraordinary woman of love and grace"

- **Dr Arun Viswanath, Vice President, Givaudan Fragrances, Singapore**

"A writer only begins a book, but a reader finishes it. 'Jasmine - Your fragrance lingers', is a meaningful reflection and articulation of a mother's love and the grief of her loss. Rachel highlights the value of the powerful presence of love. She infuses hope in the reader, to embrace pain and find meaning in grief. Reading this book has helped me unlock my own grief and has strengthened my will to find meaning in my grief and fulfil my God-given purpose in my life. This book has inspired and ministered to me in ways I did not expect".

- **Renuga Thilagaraj, Chennai, India**

"As a psychotherapist and a doting daughter, Rachel skilfully uses her own experience of grief and weaves together her experiential knowledge of psychotherapy, and biblical truth to present a perspective of gratitude and hope without denying the pain of loss and despair. This book captures the essence of 'Jasmine' as a mother and gives the reader, permission to not only experience but to embrace the process of grieving and arrive at a place of beauty and peace. I wholeheartedly recommend this book to everyone who needs comfort and healing in their own navigation of grief and to those seeking to support another in their grief".

- **Martin Gaunt, Team Manager, Adult Social Care, UK**

PREFACE

One of the most beautiful words one will ever hear in any language is the word 'mother', 'amma' in Tamil and 'momma' in English. Interestingly, in most languages, the sound of the letter 'm' is prominent in the word mother, because that is one of the first sounds babies make. The meaning of the word mother in its origin was 'that which has given birth'. I have only just uncovered the truth that during her lifetime, my mother gave birth to the transformation of many young men and women. She neither wrote books, nor ran workshops on how to love. She did not preach or sing about love. She just loved, unselfishly. Her love was no ordinary love. It was a sacrificial love, a love that never counted the cost, a love borne out of her own pain.

In the Hebrew language, the word mother translates into the words 'womb' and 'bond'. My sister and I, we were blessed to be conceived within her womb, and bonded with her, but through her natural ability to nurture and care, I now know that many who encountered her in their lives formed a bond with my mother. Her love was always a gentle but powerful force that propelled many into their destiny.

Jasmine, my mother was not necessarily streetwise, nor was she a high achiever. She was sharp-witted, intelligent, intuitively perceptive, and lovingly sensitive. She was a simple homemaker whose tender unconditional love was all anyone would need, to carry through life's everyday challenges.

In writing this book, I have drawn from my own life world as I grew up, my faith in God my Creator, my professional knowledge and experience as a Psychotherapist, and my understanding of existential philosophy. Most importantly, I draw from the source of my mother's love for me and for those around her.

This book is not merely an account of my grief of losing my mother. It documents the tremendous courage of a woman who in the face of relentless suffering and pain, poured out a love that knew no bounds. She loved everyone who knew her and forgave everyone who offended her. Even as she lay on her sick bed, she was a pillar of strength and a source of wisdom to all around her.

My heartfelt desire is to let this precious love continue to flow into the hearts of those who knew her and those who did not know her. There is something about her existence that is so meaningful that death cannot annihilate it.

DEDICATION

This book is dedicated to the most gentle, compassionate, tender hearted, kind, loving, generous and amazingly brave person, I have known since the day I was born until this very moment in time: my mother. My mentor, my role model, my best friend and my cheer leader, she is what most people who know her, describe as 'beautiful, inside-out'. Her beauty was one of a meek and a gentle spirit on the inside and a delicately charming beauty on the outside that assured you of her love every time she looked at you.

ACKNOWLEDGEMENTS

To my Creator, my Heavenly Father, for inspiring me to write this book, without His inspiration, this would not be a reality.

To Benjamin, my only child, blessed with intelligence and wisdom par excellence, who designed this book, my deepest love and gratitude.

To John, my husband, my rock, without whom I could not have weathered the storm of losing my mother.

To my patients, the wonderful people I work with, who graciously acknowledged that I too am a human being who needed to work through my own grief.

To my friends Dr Arun Viswanath and Sowmya Ramanathan, who walked with me, my journey of writing this book right from the start to the finish line. They instilled a confidence I did not have, read my manuscript, challenged me, and consistently encouraged me to endeavour.

To my cousins Pastor Simon and Ida who supported and stood by my dad at the time when my mother breathed her last and he was on his own, completely shattered. They continually offered their prayer support throughout the time of my mother's illness. To all my family and friends who offered their support and love at this very difficult time, my deepest gratitude.

Most importantly, to my mother without whose unconditional love I could not have made it to where I am today. She has been my earthly source of strength all my life. She will continue to be, for as long as I am alive. She is the reason for the 'hope' that her life through this book can offer.

PROLOGUE

Jasmine Wilhelmina is the daughter of William and Adeline Moses, the seventh of eight children, born into a typical Christian middle-class Indian family, in Jolarpettai, a village near Chennai, India. She was very shy as a child but nevertheless loving and helpful as her brothers and sisters often talked about. She was very attached to her mother and spent many hours helping her with the household chores and taking care of her siblings. Although she only achieved a secondary school leaving certificate (SSLC) which is equivalent to 'GCSE' in the UK, she would always want a scientific explanation behind concepts, never blindly accepted theories. As a young person, I remember thinking, 'my mother should have been a scientist'. Tamil was her mother tongue, but she could speak Telugu and Malayalam, the three distinct languages in south India.

The name 'Jasmine', which is of Persian origin, means *"gift from God"*. It symbolises love, purity, modesty, hospitality, community, inspiration, and spiritual ascension. Any other name would not have described my mother as accurately. She was an epitome of *love* in all its *purity*, *modest* in how she clothed herself and modest in her attitude of humility, *hospitable* even if it meant sacrificing her time. She loved being with and giving to the larger *community*. She distributed clothes and household articles to many needy people. She would take time to listen, no matter how busy she was and who it was that needed her attention, whether rich or poor. In loving the unlovable and forgiving the unforgiveable, she achieved *spiritual ascension*. She is indeed a *gift from God* and will continue to *inspire* many.

My mother Jasmine was raised by parents who loved their children very dearly but sadly, she witnessed her mother being abused by her father and grew up traumatised by this. However, when my grandfather turned his life over to God, he was transformed. He then demonstrated his tender loving care to his wife, children and grandchildren. We, my sister and cousins, grew up oblivious to what my mother and her siblings experienced early in life, but were blessed by very loving and caring grandparents who had a strong influence on all our lives.

Although my mother could see the change in her father, I know that she had not processed the trauma she experienced in the developmental years of her life, in a way we now know is crucial to mental health. I believe she carried some of that pain all her life, perhaps unconsciously.

When my mother Jasmine (Jessy) was only 18, my father who was the cousin of her sister's husband met her and it was love at first sight. He was only 23 and my mother 18 when they married. Although my father was employed at this time, he only earned a meagre wage and they struggled to make ends meet but my mother told me that it was her mother who supported them in every way possible. This is demonstrative of the typical Indian culture wherein 'family orientation' allows for married children to be supported by their parents if they needed it. My mother had a wonderful role model, in her mother. I was blessed to have my grandmother in my life until I was twenty-six years old, she was my mentor too.

My mother once told me about the time, just before they were engaged to be married, my dad would sneak in to see her. It was not permitted as per the Indian custom in their time, for couples (before betrothal) to spend time with each other privately. She said she would wonder why, when he sneaked in to see her, there was the scent of a flower she could smell. When she questioned him about it, he would pull out a string of jasmine flowers that he had bought for her, tucked away into his back pocket. Did he need to sneak in jasmine flowers to woo his beloved jasmine? I wonder! It appears that somehow my dad hoped no one would see the jasmine flowers he had hidden in his pocket! Perhaps in his enthusiasm to win the beautiful damsel he had fallen in love with, he had forgotten that flowers may not be seen but their powerful scent could easily give them away.

The jasmine flower has a distinct sweet scent. My mother can never be seen in her physical form ever again, but the fragrance she left behind, is spreading its distinct aroma, it will continue to. She cannot be hidden because the sweet scent of her love is too strong and powerful. The 'jasmine' flower is not only fragrant but is beautiful too. On her wedding day, my mother never visited a beauty parlour. She did not need to!

26th September 1963, Chennai, India

Jasmine & Livingstone

Then, the Lord God said, it is not good that man should be alone: I will make him a helper, fit for him.

Genesis 2:18

1. Crushed, but not Defeated

We may encounter many defeats, but we must refuse to be defeated

Maya Angelou

Papa?

"I think mommy is feeling very cold, we are trying to cover her but ...

She is so cold"

"Oh, mommy is not breathing, I don't think"

Can you check her pulse Papa?

"There is no pulse, no pulse at all". Her whole body feels cold suddenly, not sure what is happening. I've been here all night – holding her hand, I am calling her, but she will not respond. She always responds to me"

No Papa No?

The Thing I Feared Most

This was the chilling conversation I had with papa, my dad in Chennai, India, in the early hours (Indian time) of the 31st of March 2022. This is the moment my body began to shake uncontrollably as I was feeling shock, fear, panic, and indescribable pain, sensing my mother, is no longer with us.

This was the one call I dreaded all my life. It was here now, I had to face it. I could not evade it. I wanted to scream, cry out aloud but there was no sound. I found myself still. There were a million 'whys' bubbling up in my heart, so many of them all at the same time, that they choked me. I could not cry. I felt frozen, not knowing what my future held for me, now that my mother was gone. Was it separation anxiety? I wasn't sure. I felt crushed into a million pieces and did not know quite what to do.

My mother, she was the source of my strength. As a child and a growing up young adult, she was the one who gave me reason to believe in myself. She was the only one who praised me, encouraged me, motivated me to keep climbing, keep aspiring. She never at any time, gave me reason to believe that I should be afraid or anxious about anything. Even when I made mistakes, my mom never made me feel ashamed. She gently chastised me but never made me feel like I was a failure, just because I failed. She was, indeed, my anchor. Suddenly, it felt like my anchor was washed away.

It was the 30th of March 2022, about 8 pm (English time), when I finished my work, showered and was walking out of my shower, I felt in my spirit, a need to 'kneel down and pray for my mother'. I knelt down but began to shake, it felt like a vibration inside of me. I wondered why I was shaking. It wasn't cold, so what was it? I prayed but felt an inexplicable discomfort in my chest. I tried my best to shake off what felt very uncomfortable but could not. I then got up and made my way downstairs so I could finish my bed-time routine. This is when papa called me.

I have lived in the UK since the year I was married (2000) and have only been able to visit my parents once every year. As a young person, I never wanted to live away from my parents. I have always wanted the privilege of taking care of my parents, and so, I did not really want to live outside of India. But life's choices do not always align with some of our own desires. However, I now know that my move here was God's plan, and I will continue to be, where God wants me to be. I have learned that, when we align ourselves with God's plan in where He wants us to be located, then life will be purposeful and fulfilling, with the opportunities and the people He will position for us.

When Your Spirit is Attuned to the One You Love

I did not know it, but I was in communion with my Creator, just as my mother's soul departed from her body, the body of the woman who had borne me, nursed me, cradled me, nurtured me, the woman without whom I would not be here. I knew then, my life would never be the same again.

This explained the peculiar sensation in my body at the time I knelt down to pray. My human spirit was intuitively reacting in my body, to the spirit of my mother that was departing from her body. After all, my body was part of hers' before I stepped out into the world. And because my love for her was very deep and I was very close to her, my spirit was attuned to hers in a way I could not describe.

I have a profession that I find deeply meaningful, a beautiful family, blessed with a fulfilling ministry, and yet at this precise moment it felt like my whole entire world had crumbled. I had nothing left to live for. Suddenly, nothing made sense.

I had never felt more crushed in my spirit than at this moment. I was crushed to the very core of my being. Suddenly, I felt like I was drowning, in a flood of emotions, unanswered questions and inexplicable pain. Will I ever find the strength to stand on my feet again and move on, I wondered? Will I ever smile again?

I remember arriving in Chennai and walking out of the airport, tears streaming down my face, seeing large numbers of people eagerly looking for their loved ones, and I heard this scream inside of me 'do you know why I have arrived here, I have come to bury my mother, do you even know what that feels like'? Deep inside of me, I felt angry at the whole world, angry at God, for suddenly taking away from me, the one person who truly loved and cared about me.

When I arrived at my parents' home from the airport, the house was full of people, but it felt empty, it did not feel like home. Even when mom was bed bound and asleep a lot of the time, her presence made a difference. In her presence was a love that could not be measured or described.

> **Love has a presence, a powerfully undeniable presence.**

Mom and Dad in UK, 2003

An excellent wife who can find. She is far more precious than jewels. The heart of her husband trusts in her, and he will have no lack of gain. She does him good, and not harm, all the days of her life

Proverbs 31:1

Mom & Dad leaving the UK after their first visit in 2004

She watches over the affairs of her household and does not eat the bread of idleness

Proverbs 31:27

Later that day, as my mother's body was being lowered into her grave, I thought I was going to collapse, she was my human source of strength, and I would never have her look of approval or hear her loving gentle voice ever again. As her coffin quickly receded into the ground, I stood there, wondering how I was going to face life without her. I wished I could disappear too, with her but that was the moment I heard these words in my spirit: *"You can either let your sorrow drown you or you can allow it to lift you up, to carry on her legacy"*

This as I know now, was the voice of my Creator, God Himself. I knew then that, in order to make the choice of carrying on her legacy, I would have to let go of my mother, and surrender her into the arms of my Creator. There was no other way I could make her life count. It was difficult to let go, but once I did it, it felt like I was ready to pick up where mom left.

A Paradigm Shift

The moment that my mother's body began to descend into the ground, became the moment, my life changed. At this moment, I caught a glimpse of the cover of this book, in my mind's eye, and instantly felt a deep stirring within me, to write this book. I knew it was God stirring up my spirit. Suddenly, I felt my strength was renewed. My life suddenly felt it had new meaning and purpose. My life now after my mother's life here on earth, will never be the same. My worldview, my outlook of life, my attitude towards who I really am, has changed forever. "It's *when I struggle that I strengthen. It's when challenged to the core that I learn the depth of who I am*" Steve Maraboli.

This is a fundamental change in my approach to life, a paradigm shift. It is this shift that is empowering me each day. Wintley Phipps (founder of the American Dream Academy) said "*It is in the quiet crucible of your personal and private suffering that your noblest dreams are born, and God's greatest gifts are given, in compensation to what you've been through*". I know this was the moment my dream to spread the love of God, my Creator, with my God given potential, would be fulfilled, through the life and love of my mother.

Life sometimes allows for suffering that will tear your soul. But it is when your heart is shattered and your soul torn apart, that, the underlying distorted beliefs are revealed. It is this same 'shattering' that helps you discover the God-given hidden treasure of your potential within. I say 'hidden' because, often, life's challenges and pain layer the inner core of our 'being' and we lose sight of what God has placed within us. Many of my patients have said to me "I don't think I know who I really am".

> **Not knowing who we really are, is the greatest error of omission we can ever make, as it can deny us of our destination.**

In the last five years of her life, mom progressively lost her mobility due to her auto-immune disorder. In the last two years of her life, she struggled to walk, to stand up in the kitchen, to cook. Cooking food and serving her family and anyone who came to visit her, was one of her greatest joys. In serving others, she served God. She would gladly rearrange her plans if someone unexpectedly dropped in to visit them. Hospitality was a unique God-given gift, which was really, her ministry, her way of sowing into others' lives. It pained her that she could no longer serve people. But that did not stop her from loving or serving. She always made sure that whoever came to visit them, had a drink or even food to eat, more importantly, a listening ear if they needed one.

The suffering she had to endure in her body never eased at any time. She often told us that she was a burden because she became dependent on others, even for the little things she needed. I always responded saying, it was our privilege to take care of her, but she could never see it that way. She often whispered in pain; she had no energy to cry. As her pain progressed and we were no longer able to control it despite medication, we knew she felt crushed not just physically, but also emotionally and mentally, caused by her belief that she was a burden.

While her body became weaker and weaker, her soul was emerging stronger. Despite her pain, she always had a word of encouragement and wise counsel if we needed it. Her pain never stopped her from smiling, the smile that could light up any heart.

> **'Crushing' is an act, but 'defeat' is an attitude**

I often noticed that my mother was shattered and appeared subdued but would not surrender to defeat. Oftentimes, she felt struck down but would not be destroyed. She continuously forgave those who offended her. On her sick bed, she prayed for all those who persecuted her and blessed all those who cursed her and in doing so, she won the final victory.

My mother experienced a crushing through many parts of her life. In the final lap of the race of her life, her failing physical health compounded it all, but she still refused to accept defeat.

Bishop T D Jakes, one of my all-time favourite speakers and authors, in his book 'Crushing' said: *"Crushing could occur through life's deepest heartaches and most devastating disappointments, but it is not the end. It is only the beginning"*.

Through allowing for the crushing, my mother produced sweet wine. Her crushing was not the end. She, 'the grape' is no longer here but she left behind, for us, the wine she produced through her crushing. She exists, only now, in the form of sweeter wine. The essence of her fruit is here and will continue to enrich our lives.

With Benjamin on his 18th Birthday, August 2021

Though the fig tree shall not blossom, neither shall fruit be on the vines; the produce of the olive shall fail, and the fields shall yield no meat; the flock shall be cut off from the fold, and there shall be no herd in the stalls. Yet I will rejoice in the Lord, I will take joy in the God of my salvation.

Habakkuk 3:17-18

'Antimony' a chemical element of atomic number 51, a brittle silvery white metalloid, in ancient times, which did not burn easily was powdered and used as a medicine. In the last five years of her life, my mother Jasmine was crushed to her core, but the crushing only brought forth more of her unconditional love, even towards those who cursed her. It is this 'love' that became a healing balm to us, as we felt crushed, just watching her suffer. No offensive word or act could burn or consume her from within. The more she was crushed, the more the essence of her sacrificial love, the more compassion.

I am crushed not because I have lost the one source of love in its purest form but because I could not take away her pain and her suffering. However, I refuse to be defeated, because I know God did what I could not do, He took away all her pain and set her free, the moment He called her home to Himself.

> **If left unattended, a broken heart can cause a sense of feeling lost in the dark, the darkness of sorrow and despair, resulting with a darkness of the soul.**

But, just as it did for my mother, crushing for me, comes with a price. The loss of my mother wounded my spirit. A wound is an injury, usually a physical one. But a wounded spirit is a crushed soul caused by a broken heart. *(The Lord is close to the broken hearted and saves those who are crushed in the spirit Psalm 34:18).*

2. Darkness can Produce Light

The wound is the place where light enters you

Rumi

I never knew that the dark places of life could produce strength, wisdom and light, until I saw my mother navigate some of the darkest paths of her life and through witnessing her illness and then losing her, I had to navigate a dark path in my own life.

In the last five years of her life, my mother was afflicted in her body and wounded in her spirit, but throughout her life, she suffered emotional distress. Despite pouring out her love unconditionally, my mother had been cursed and rejected by some of the very people she loved dearly. She was emotionally and mentally oppressed. These were the works of darkness. I knew she was deeply saddened by this but when I tried to talk about her emotional pain, she would always say that whoever said or did something that offended her, did so, out of their own inadequacies and pain, and so, she would choose to forgive them. My mother had the supernatural ability to absorb offence and radiate love, unconditional love towards the person offending her, without any bitterness or resentment.

I understood then that darkness could not penetrate her heart, she was like the 'carbuncle', a gemstone, commonly known as a 'red garnet' that can provide its own illumination to an otherwise dark interior. It emits light even in total darkness. An old English translation describes the carbuncle as 'a gemstone that makes it day when the day is gone because of the light it produced'. In her illness, my mother appeared to live in the darkness of disability and pain. However, through her attitude of love, she emitted light, even in darkness. The light she produced did not go out when her day was gone, it shines brighter. *"There are some who bring a light so great to the world that even after they have gone, the light remains"* - anonymous

The Formation of Gemstones

Some of the most precious gemstones are formed only within volcanoes and metamorphic rocks, radiating a wide variety of colours. The pain caused in my mother's life through the volcanic eruptions of anger and words of curses that were flung on her like metamorphic rocks did not break or destroy her but transformed her into a gemstone. She had the ability to refract any darkness around her and radiate light. She was the red garnet who had the ability to shine her light even amid the darkness of her physical and emotional afflictions.

My mother Jasmine was deeply loved and admired by innumerable people who looked up to her as their own mother/sister/friend, but she became a multi-faceted gemstone only through the many volcanic eruptions of envy, anger, hatred and curse, radiating a light that surpassed darkness. Like the 'red garnet' stone that 'in the end, will always make it day, when the day is gone', my mother's light continues to shine even after her day is gone.

> **God needs no light, to produce light. He can use the darkest moment of our life to produce light.**

It seems that in our attempt to love unconditionally and give generously, we can sometimes be hated and rejected, and we will suffer. It is in this darkness of suffering, pain and rejection that purpose and strength can be borne. It is now my privilege, to ignite that same light into the souls of others but emerging from darkness into light is a process, one of suffering and pain.

3. Pain can Disable or Enable

Pain & Suffering are the dark strands
through the tapestry of your life, providing
the shadows that give depth and dimension
to the masterpiece God is fashioning
within you

Joseph Girzone

One evening, I called, just to say goodnight to mom, which I did every night. But on this occasion, I could not talk to her as she was busy talking to her caretaker on the phone. I asked my dad why she was talking to her caretaker at that time of the day as she had been there all day. My dad told me that the caretaker had not come in that day as she was not well, and my mother had called to check on her. My mother herself was in pain but somehow, she would always reach out to those that were struggling in any way, to see if they needed something she could offer. It did not matter to her that she was in pain. She was always able to look past her own pain to reach out to another. Pushing past her own pain to touch another in pain was a gift my mother seemed to have been bestowed with, by her Creator.

This is what my mother's younger sister told me:

"I often think of our days together. She used to take good care of me when I was a little child. She herself was little, and she used to love me. My young days with her were lovely. She never retaliated, never harboured bitterness. Even though she had her own homework to do, she used to teach me and help me with mine"
-Tulip

I have, many a time wondered how my mother was able to live her life, given the daily hardships and the emotional pain, she suffered. She was able to pour out her love, not only on her own family but on everyone else she knew. It is evident to me now that it was the strength and power of the love, she had for others that enabled her to endure her own pain and emerge stronger. (*Love is patient, love is kind. It does not envy, it does not boast, it is not proud. It is not rude, it is not self-seeking, it is not easily angered, it keeps no account of wrongs. Love takes no pleasure in evil but rejoices in the truth. It bears all things, believes all things, hopes all things, endures all things.* 1 Corinthians 13:4-7) The 'love' that empowered my mother to bear all things despite her pain, enabled her to reach out to those in need around her.

As a family, we met virtually, every single day, to pray together, to nourish my mother's soul. In so doing, we nourished one another, deepening our own roots of faith. As we prayed together, mom would faithfully sit up at prayer time. She not only joined us to listen but also prayed herself. She thanked and praised God with us, while she suffered intense debilitating pain.

I was in a church service one Sunday morning, not long after my mother passed away and found myself crying. I had my head bowed and was not looking around. Suddenly, I found a hand, held out to me with a tissue. I thought, 'oh someone has observed me crying'. Then I looked at the person whose hand it was - it was someone who was physically incapacitated. Was it perhaps, his own affliction that enhanced his sensitivity to observe and understand another's pain? Instead of allowing his pain to disable him, he used it to enable him to reach out to another. It was such a simple gesture of thoughtful compassion, it touched me, it comforted me.

The Gift of 'Listening'

Just after we had buried my mother, I met several people who were weeping bitterly, in sorrow. I had the privilege of talking to some. They were the caregivers, the cleaners, the gardener, the plumber, the carpenter, the tailor, the neighbour, the tenants, the vegetable vendors, they were all people who had been deeply touched by my mother in some way. They all said the same thing: *"Amma always listened to my problems, even though she herself was in pain. She was the person I could cry to. I always felt encouraged after I spoke to amma. She was like a mother to me"*

I have seen my mother talk to people who came to work in the house, but I did not know that she took time to listen to everyone, individually. Her conversations were neither casual nor superficial. She had the ability to make anyone who encountered her, feel special and important, listened to, and understood, no matter how good or bad, rich or poor, young or old they were.

I find it hard to comprehend how, while my mother's pain was physically disabling, spiritually, it enabled her to overflow with a love so tender and so sweet. What was it about her that gave her this secret power? It seems she had a secret source of joy.

She crossed the finish line with great pain but triumphed with unspeakable joy

4. Joy is a Given, Happiness is a Choice

While, happiness doesn't depend on any external conditions and is governed by our mental attitude (Dale Carnegie), Joy is a spring from deep down that never runs dry no matter what happens (S D Gordon)

A few days after my mother's departure, I woke up, got out of bed, feeling excited about the ideas God placed on my heart, to carry on the legacy mom left behind. I felt a warmth in my heart but then, at the same time, felt a deep sadness, wondering 'will I be happy ever again?' This felt painful, but in some strange way, it felt comforting as it made me believe that, for as long as I allowed myself to feel the pain of my loss, I could be close to her. Suffering with the pain of my grief, would mean, I was loyal to her, that I would never allow her to be forgotten. It wasn't long before I realised, I was wrong when I heard the spirit of God speak into my spirit: *'Joy is a given, but happiness is a choice'* What was God saying to me? I believe He was saying that I was given the power of choice, and I could choose to be happy, that it was possible to be happy despite pain because happiness is produced by joy which is a 'given'. However, I need to make an intentional choice.

> **Joy is a 'given', it comes from within. Happiness is a 'choice' it is a pursuit**

What Exactly is Joy?

The Cambridge English dictionary defines 'joy' as *'great happiness and delight'* but the Greek origin of the word Joy is *'rejoice because of grace'*. Joy does bring delight, but it is different from happiness. Joy is a given because the abundant grace of God is a given. (*Rejoice in the Lord always. I will say it again: Rejoice* - Philippians 4:4). So rejoicing is only a matter of activating the joy that He has already placed within us, and His grace is sufficient.

If Joy is a 'given', why is it that some of us struggle to experience joy in our daily life? Scripture quotes in Galatians 5:22 that *'Joy' is a fruit of the spirit*. So, we, God's creation should all have joy on the inside of us, as He has breathed His spirit, His breath into us. If joy is a fruit of His Spirit in us, then His breath in us produces joy. This is what God meant when He said, 'joy' is a given. It is like a spring from deep within.

Joy, an Activation of Pain?

A natural spring occurs when water pressure causes a natural flow of groundwater onto the earth's surface. Applying the same principle, every pressure that we encounter has the potential to activate and sustain joy. (*Behold, I am about to do a new thing; now it shall spring forth, do you not perceive it? I will make a way in the wilderness and rivers in the desert.* Isaiah 43:19)

This is what my mother did, she used her incessant pain (both physical and emotional) to act as the pressure from within to bring forth her love. She only had to smile, and you would feel the warmth of her love. You would know that she has your best interest at heart. You could see that somewhere deep inside her being, there was this hidden resource, she would draw from.

'Joy', a Seed that can Produce a Fragrant Garden

Many years ago, I wrote these words on a birthday card for my mother:

Mommy:

> My life is a beautiful garden, full of fragrance
>
> It's the fragrance of your love, your every sacrifice

> The sacrifice of your deep devotion, your thoughtfulness, your care
>
> My garden was watered by your tears and nourished by
>
> Your every act of patient endurance

It was only after my mother passed away that I realised it was not just my garden she had watered, she touched everyone. Everyone who knew her was influenced by her attitude of compassion and touched by her tender loving care and affection. Every dry and parched heart was watered and nourished by her love. At the graveside, Sam (one of the young men who had rented a room in my parents' house many years ago) showed me this photograph he had captured in my parents' home:

Joy is a Given, Happiness is a Choice | **29**

Looking at a birthday card she just received, rather shocked because she is not worthy to be compared with Mother Teresa

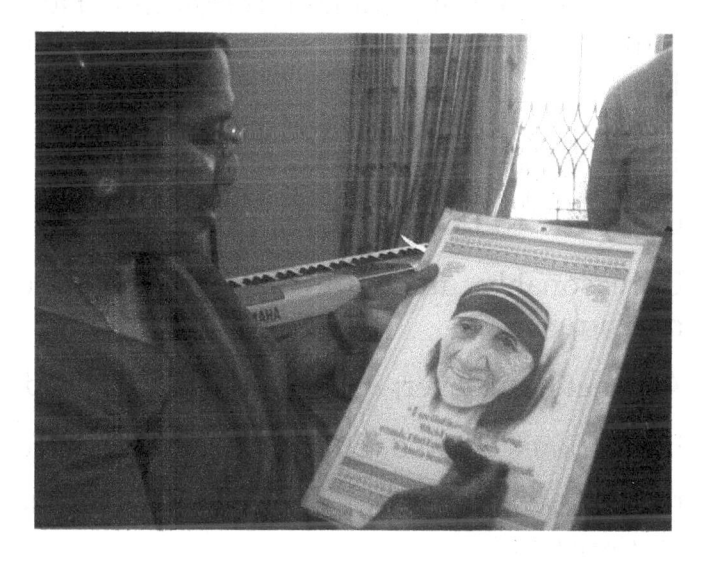

She opens her arms to the poor and extends her hands to the needy

Proverbs 31:20

As he showed me this photo, Sam said:

"Between your mother and Mother Teresa, there was really no difference".

I thought to myself, 'what is he talking about?' 'My mother was just a housewife, quietly going about her duties as a wife and a mother, how could it have been possible for her to do anything Mother Teresa did? How could he compare my mother with Mother Teresa?

These are his (Sam's) words:

Unparalleled Life, Amazing Love

Unreasonably merciful, Beautiful beyond measure

A sweet home ever; A Comforter unmatched

Industrious, Untired; Euphemistic in language

Emphatic in Approach; An incurable Optimist

A chosen vessel of God; A garden of Grace

A forgotten Pulse; A school of Love

A sweet flower enriched in fragrance

Is my pretty aunt, the prettiest ever

I will miss you forever aunty ma ...

Sam Jebadurai

My mother, I believe, tapped into the joy deep down in her heart, to produce happiness by sowing richly into the lives of the people she knew. She had to choose to be happy every day because of the adverse conditions in which she often found herself.

What is Happiness?

'Happiness' has been defined as a subjective state of pleasure and/or contentment. This means happiness is dependent on external stimuli. Does this mean that if our lifeworld, is void of stimuli to produce pleasure or contentment, then we cannot have happiness?

From a psychological perspective, happiness is a state of well-being that encompasses living a good life, one with a sense of meaning and deep contentment. It is an achievement that often involves discomfort and pain through the many challenges and finding purpose beyond oneself. Happiness does not promote well-being, it is the actual pursuit, and 'pursuing', is a choice. Happiness is unique to each one because every individual's life experience is unique. This clarifies that happiness is a choice. My mother's life was not a blissfully happy life but through her ability to love unconditionally and forgive graciously, she pursued happiness.

Can Joy and Sorrow Co-exist?

Happiness is not the absence of pain or suffering. Happiness can exist amid pain and suffering but it is a choice we each can make amid suffering. The question though is, how can we be happy and sorrowful at the same time. Can the two co-exist? I can be sad that my mother is no longer present in her body which means, I can no longer see her or be seen by her, no longer hear her gentle voice or feel her cheek against mine. But I can yet choose to be happy because she no longer suffers, on the other hand, she rejoices in the presence of her Creator, her master.

I have not lost her; I have simply lost contact with her. I can choose to be happy because she is happy, because her heavenly father has wiped away all her tears and her body is no longer in pain. This happiness that I can feel is not a default emotion.

I realise that even though I know where she is and that she is no longer suffering, it still hurts because I would rather have had her here with me, with us, even if it meant I needed to take care of her. Her love made me feel strong. Could this be selfish love? Knowing that I had her unconditional love made me courageous because it meant, I could face any challenge in life. It did not matter who rejected me or abandoned me, my mother's love was the anchor that grounded me.

What I have learned now though, is that she may be absent in her body now, but her spirit is present with the Lord. She may have died, but her love will never die. I may feel severed from her, but my love for her and her love for me can never be severed.

I am confident therefore, that happiness and sadness, joy and sorrow, can co-exist. I am happy that she is rejoicing and will forever be happy in the presence of her Creator. At the same time, I am sad that she is no longer present here with me, with us. I am happy for her, but sad for myself. Did not the hymn writer (J H Burke) say "Joy & Sorrow interwoven, Love in all I see?" Through my joy and sorrow, I feel her love, the love that continues to keep me grounded and established in who I am called to be.

The sadness is not here to live forever though, each passing day, I feel less sad, not because I do not miss her anymore, but because 'Heaven', her present residence, is just becoming a little more real to me every day.

It seems that there is something significant about a mother's unconditional love that will choose to pursue the happiness of 'giving' even amid pain and suffering.

5. A Mother's Love: What it can do

A mother's love for her child is like nothing else in the world. It knows no law, no pity. It dares all things and crushes down remorselessly all that stands in its path

Agatha Christie

What is it about a mother's love that one cannot fully grasp nor let go of? The word mother denotes 'relationship'. No matter how many relationships a woman might have, her relationship with her baby, her child, is unique, it is one she will make time for, no matter how busy or exhausted she is. It is a love relationship, a love of the purest kind. My mother loved me before I got to know her and her love grasped me in the innermost core of my being and this is how I knew she was aware of the essence of me at the core of my being and I, hers. And through our attunement with each other, our souls became intertwined. It seems that from the time I was born, I was in a secret partnership with my mother. No one quietly observed me with the kind of sensitivity that she did. No one understood and appreciated me in every aspect of my life, as she did. Even as a young child, I knew she loved me enough to correct me while applauding my accomplishments. I do not know of anyone who was as fully aware of the very essence of my being, as she was. Her love is so powerful a presence in my soul, that I cannot rip it out of my heart. It is her deep love that enabled her to know who I really am, like no one else knew me or will ever know me. Viktor Frankl, a Christian psychiatrist who experienced the extremities of human suffering in four different concentration camps, said *"No one can become fully aware of the very essence of another human being unless he loves him"*

Attachment and Self-worth

Sadly, not all of us experience a mother's love as unconditional and tender. But even when there is a lack of love or attachment between a mother and her child, there still exists, a relationship. After all, the mother bore her child in her womb and was physiologically attached to her child. Thus, the baby, through the physiological connection develops a psychological attachment and an unconditional love for the mother without a conscious awareness of it.

As a psychotherapist, I often encounter men and women, who have not had a healthy attachment with their mothers. Regardless of how rejected they felt by their mothers, these people have a deep secret longing in their hearts to re-connect with their mothers, despite a tough exterior that displays an 'I'm okay' attitude. In his book 'Momma and the Meaning of Life', Irvin Yalom, a world-renowned psychotherapist, said "*I am a writer, and my momma cannot read. Still, I turn to her for the meaning of my life's work. Every time I visited my mother, I found her in her chair with two or three of my books on her lap. She weighed them, smelled them, caressed them, everything but read them. She was blind. We are meaning-seeking creatures*".

It is fascinating, that even in the face of rejection, children seek a connection, an attachment with their mothers. It is 'attachment' that provides a secure base wherein people derive a sense of identity and self-worth.

Why is it that we human beings tie up the meaning of our life, to the security and validation our mothers can give us? From the time we are separated from our mothers' bodies, we slowly become independent of them, no matter how much we need them and how much we love them. Yet, we look to our mothers for their approval, their love and acceptance. I do not remember having in-depth, insightful conversations with my mother, that would explicitly convey affirmation or validation of my endeavours and my achievements.

My mother only had to look at me, and perhaps draw a sigh of adoration, it was all I needed to feel warmth and affection, recognition and appreciation. If ever I achieved anything, anything at all, the first person I wanted to talk about it with, was my mother. It did not have to be anything significant; she would be proud of even the smallest things I would talk about and her pride in my achievements was her pride in me. The pride I experienced through her, was often what gave me, a sense of worth. If I did not achieve something I aimed to achieve and was disappointed in myself, she would encourage me to look at my failure in a positive light. She neither put me down nor encouraged negative self-talk.

In the face of the adversities my mother experienced, she often questioned her own self-worth, but somehow, without many words at all, she made me feel proud of myself, established in me, a sense of who I really am. Do I miss what she gave me - the sense of confidence she instilled in me? Yes, I do, every moment of everyday, but I also know that just by being herself in the way she gave of her love, she gave me everything I wanted. I have learned everything I ever wanted to learn from her, received everything I ever could have received from her. Yet, I could never say 'I've had enough of my mother or that I have given enough'. Nothing I did for her feels good enough. No matter how long my mother lived, I would never feel satisfied with the love I received from her. I would have selfishly wanted more and to give more.

However, it has taken me all this time to discover that she did not take away with her, the love she had in her heart for me, she left it all behind. Now, I realise that I love her enough, to let her go, let her rest, and so I have. After all, she loved me and trusted me enough, to live my life without her, but not just that,to carry on loving.

> **A mother's love is tender and yet tough; soft yet firm; it can let go and yet sustain. It is the only love that can hold you while at the same time, give you a sense of self**

Mom, Dad, Me & my sister with her son Joel Isaac, 2000

She opens her mouth with wisdom, and on her tongue is the law of kindness.

Proverbs 31:26

Graduation – UK, 2018

For you formed my inward parts; You knit me together in my mother's womb. I will give thanks to you, for I am fearfully and wonderfully made

Psalm 139:13

Daniel Stern (1985), explained that the way in which a mother interacts with her baby synchronising her interactions through recognising, validating and communicating her feelings without necessarily using words, is how she tunes into her baby's feelings in a resting state. This interaction produced by her atonement is what contributes to the development of the baby's capacity to feel, giving him a subjective sense of self.

My mother was only 19 years of age when she gave birth to me, under circumstances of acute financial strain. My parents' finances were extremely limited, but nothing hindered my mother from tuning into mine and my sister's emotional needs to ensure we felt comfortable and secure.

Many years later, she mothered her grandsons, giving them too, a love and affection so deep and so tender that they feel just as attached to their grandmother as to their own mothers. Their attachment with her is as strong as mine and my sister's, to our mother. She loved them with a grandmother's tenderness and yet taught them with a mother's firm resoluteness.

Holding her first grandson Joel Isaac

Her children arise and call her blessed

Proverbs 31:28

Joel Isaac with his beloved grandmother

Listen, my son, to your father's instruction; and don't reject your mother's teaching, for they will be a garland of grace on your head and a gold chain around your neck.

Proverbs 1: 8-9

A Mother's Love: What it can do | **45**

Beaming with happiness as she holds her second grandson Benjamin

She sets about her work vigorously; her arms are strong for her tasks

Proverbs 31:17

Benjamin with his beloved grandmother

Honour your father and your mother, as the Lord your God has commanded you, that your days may be long and that it may be well with you in the land which the Lord is giving you.

Deuteronomy 5:16

Without her being aware of it, my mother gave her children and her grandchildren, a strong sense of self through the secure attachment her unconditional love provided.

> **A mother's love transports belief in 'self', one's sense of worth**

A Secure Attachment

A 'secure attachment' is developed by the child having primary caregivers who are positively attuned to the child, with care, affection, and attention, providing a consistent safety. These children grow to boldly explore the world and interact with others with trust, building emotional resilience. – Dr Diane Heller

It is my mother's unconditional love that developed in me, the courage to explore my 'self' and my 'world', building in me, the ability to be emotionally sensitive, empathic and understanding. It is her love that transported into me, my sense of self-worth, although her own self-worth had not been developed in a healthy manner, in the early years of her life.

Here is another narrative by one of the young men that rented a room in the house.

"I am honoured to tell you about Jessy aunty, an exceptional woman I met in my life, who cared about me like she was my own mother. She treated everyone like her own, her door was always open to everyone. She was like a second mother to many, and to some the mother they themselves did not have. I remember sitting many times and talking for hours with her. She always had great stories and advice. Her words of admonishment and encouragement were directly from Heaven. She knew how to comfort those who were going through trials and tribulations. Her labour of love and the many fruits this bore in the body of Christ will be a living testimony for ever. She was a very loving woman with a beautiful soul. She patiently taught me many things. Most importantly, her love and support and hospitality for our 'youth fellowship' was a great blessing to many young people who gathered in Jessy aunt's home. She may be gone from our midst, but she can never ever go out of our hearts" -Anish Kumar

The Youth Fellowship facilitated by Mom & Dad in their home

"I cannot forget the days we spent in the Sundar Nagar home. Jessy aunty was a God-given mother for us who showed unconditional love to us and supported our youth fellowship"

Anish Kumar

My mother sowed precious seeds of love and care, not only into her children and grandchildren's lives but into the lives of many others. One did not have to be her child, to be loved and cared for. There was no difference in the way she loved her own children and those of others. There never was favouritism of any kind.

It seems that my mother's impartial, altruistic, consistent love has provided many young people, a secure attachment which has established a sense of identity and confidence in themselves, in who they really are.

We, every one of us, can be a mother, a father, a sister, a brother, a grandparent, a friend to someone in need of love and compassion. As we look around us, we can see: *"There is more hunger for love and appreciation in this world than for bread. Even the rich are hungry for love, for being cared for, for being wanted, for having someone to call their own."* – Mother Teresa

Love Replenished

When we donate blood, our body becomes overdriven, to replenish it. The human body produces two million new red blood cells every second. So it is with love, it never depletes when given away. My mother proved it.

> **Love given away is not lost, it is replenished in abundance.**

I know my mother's love has been my one consistent source of happiness and has given me a sense of confidence in who I am but how do I intentionally pursue happiness when it's very source feels severed?

6. Love Activates Joy; Joy Produces Happiness

Not all of us can do great things but we can all do small things with great love

Mother Teresa

My mother, She:

Never wrote books nor composed songs

She never ran a charity

Nor staged motivational talks

With all the limitations of her own life

She cared deeply about

Every soul she encountered

She loved everyone that knew her

Expecting nothing in return

She was never applauded by anyone

Never won a noble prize

No matter what little she did

She did with great love

That's what makes this simple quiet unassuming woman

A truly honourable woman – my Mother

"What's the big deal here, everyone loses their parents eventually. Why all this hue and cry about my loss and my pain. Everyone suffers when they lose a parent. Isn't this life?" … is perhaps a question in your mind, as you read this?

When a person who has occupied a large part of your heart and life suddenly moves away, the heart feels empty and the suffering unbearable.

True, my mother was just another ordinary housewife who raised her children and her grandchildren, served her parents, her family and community like most women do. But then, she was the ordinary woman who accomplished extraordinary tasks. She loved the unlovable and reached out to the poorest of the poor, forgave the unforgivable, in a way that most people could not. She never compared herself or competed with anyone else. She never ever complained, even when she suffered acute pain. She was the best she could be in the way she was called to be. She may have done only little things, but she did it with great love. Her seemingly insignificant life has made such a great big impact, that I could not sit still and do nothing about it. The purpose of bringing her life to light, is to allow the light of her selfless unconditional love to continue to activate joy and inspire those who knew her and those who are yet to know her.

My mother was a living expression of kindness, she did not have to say much, or do much, but there was kindness in her face, in her eyes, in her smile, it was a kindness that was borne out of love, a love that knew no bounds. Her spirit of humility and gentleness always adorned her.

Love Activates Joy; Joy Produces Happiness | **55**

In the middle of her busy day at home in Chennai

But let your adorning be the hidden person of the heart with the imperishable beauty of a gentle and quiet spirit, which in God's sight is very precious.

1 Peter 3:4

Although I lived far away from my parents, it never felt like I was separated from them as I would talk to them at least twice every day. I made it a point to talk to them every day so I could in some small way, support them but even when my mother was ill, I was able to draw strength from her as her love was relentless and had no pity on herself. Her love stirred up the joy in me, the joy that gave me strength. But when I knew, I could no longer talk to her, it felt like my life purpose was threatened. I felt like my one source of happiness was cut off. I had no hope left.

Why I was Afraid to Lose My Mother

Death is the one certainty about life, but despite anticipating the end, our whole system, both physical and mental, responds with shock when the end does come. My greatest fear in losing my mother was that I would lose my fulfilment of loving and serving her, of receiving her love. But it did not take me long, to know that I was wrong. As I positioned myself to continue spreading the fragrance of my mother's love, I recognised that I would be finding fulfilment in carrying her legacy. This recognition activates my joy and produces a deep sense of happiness, a happiness that is derived from a sense of fulfilment.

"Love goes far beyond the physical person of the beloved. It finds its deepest meaning in his

spiritual being, his inner self. Whether or not, he is actually present, whether or not, he is still alive at all, ceases somehow to be of importance"
Viktor Frankl

As much as I yearn for my mother's look of love and approval, it does not matter anymore that she is no longer present in her body because her love has penetrated deeply into my heart and the hearts of people, near and far. It is her love that has taken root and borne fruit. My deepest meaning now is in my inner being, my soul, being nourished so that my mother's love, through my own soul, can continue to flow into the hearts of those she knew and those that are yet to know her. It is this joy that propels me into creating something so meaningful and purposeful that I can say, I am fulfilled and happy.

Love and Joy: Intricately Connected

If joy is the natural spring that is at the core of my being, then the pain of losing my mother has become the pressure that brings out my potential to activate joy. I realise that if I choose to use my pain to act as the pressure to activate my joy, then I have chosen to be happy. The happiness I am referring to here is derived from the fulfilment of finding meaning in my grief. Grief may produce sorrow and pain, but it is the 'meaning' that produces fulfilment and happiness, offering a reason to move forward.

If you are touched by her love and will carry that same love in your heart, then she is your mother too.

> **A mother's love activates joy but sharing this joy can spread happiness, even in the face of adversity**

Scientists have now discovered that the human brain is wired for love and wired to love. This is in alignment with the bible (*God has not given us a spirit of fear, but of power, of love, and of a sound mind.* 2 Timothy 1:7). When God breathed His breath into us, He breathed His love, His power, imparting His mind too. After all, *"He made us in His own image"*. (Genesis 1:27).

Love, therefore, is the essence of the ultimate fulfilment of life. But how do we find any meaning in life when it appears we have lost the greatest source of love?

7. Finding Meaning in Grief

In some ways, suffering ceases to be suffering at the moment it finds a meaning, such as the meaning of a sacrifice

Viktor Frankl

As I write this book, I think, I reflect, I hurt, I weep, but I carry on writing. I feel an indescribable pain, the pain of my grief. It is however fascinating that it is in the writing, that I am facilitating the processing of my grief. As I process my grief through my writing, my grief is being transformed into something rich and fulfilling. This is the meaning I find in my grief. Through my meaning-making, I am being healed. The meaning is in the delight of carrying my mother's love in my heart and sharing it. Perhaps this is what Paulo Coelho meant when he said, *"What hurts us is what heals us"*.

The question though is, how can suffering be meaningful? We probably ask ourselves questions such as: Who am I? What is the purpose of my life? Why am I here on this earth? What is the meaning of my life? Why do I have to suffer?

To find 'meaning' in suffering and grief, is to find a reason to exist. There would be no suffering if there was no life, there would be no life if there was no existence. So, what does it mean to exist?

Understanding Existence

To exist is to have an entity, an essence, a substance in the individuality of one's being, of body, mind, and soul. Existence therefore cannot be described without a purpose, without an essence. Neither can existence exist without suffering and pain. Often, it is in the suffering and in the pain, that meaning is derived. Therefore, it is imperative that we embrace suffering.

Emmy Van Deurzen, a clinical psychologist & philosopher said:

"When people rediscover their inner connectedness to something greater than themselves, to some ideal which will lift them beyond their everyday struggles, a new motivation flows inside of them, which can carry them through difficulties with unerring purposefulness"

This draws attention to the fundamental need for purposefulness in life, in all its dimensions of existence. This 'unerring purposefulness', cannot be discovered, without an inner connectedness to something greater than the human self. It is necessary then, for a conscious awareness of what it is that is greater than us, human beings, that we should be connected with.

Research demonstrates that infant-parent bond or a sense of connection/attachment provides a security that increases resilience and improves mental health. Interactions with available and supportive attachment figures impart a sense of safety, trigger positive emotions, and provide emotional strength for dealing with problems and adversities. People who feel secure remain undisturbed during times of stress and recover faster from distress. This contributes to their overall emotional well-being and mental health. (*Official Journal of the World Psychiatric Association, 2012*)

What is it about 'connection' that provides meaning and purpose? In their research article 'The Connection Prescription: Using the power of social interactions and the deep desire for connectedness to empower health and wellness', Martino, Pegg and Pegg Frates, write that there is significant evidence to prove that human beings are wired to connect and this connection can help people maintain blood sugar levels, improve cancer survival, decrease cardiovascular mortality, reduce stress, improve self-esteem, decrease depressive symptoms and enhance overall mental health.

If connecting with people can empower human beings to maintain a healthy and sound body and mind, then what would a connection with someone greater than the human self, mean, for the development of a healthy sense of self?

Connection with God = Connection with Self

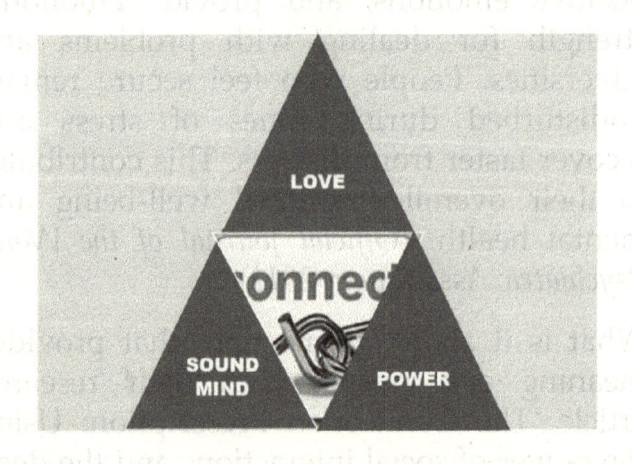

Because it is God who breathed His breath into us, we are, by default, connected with Him. But often, the 'givens' of our life cause us to lose sight of this connection. Therefore, it is crucial for us as human beings to be consciously aware of our need for this connection. Our consciousness of our Creator and our connection with Him, is in effect, the consciousness of, and connection with, our 'self'.

In order not to lose sight of this connection with 'self', it is imperative we understand the dimensions of our existence that layer our sense of 'self', our inner self.

Dimensions of Human Existence

Human existence is composed of different dimensions, as illustrated below:

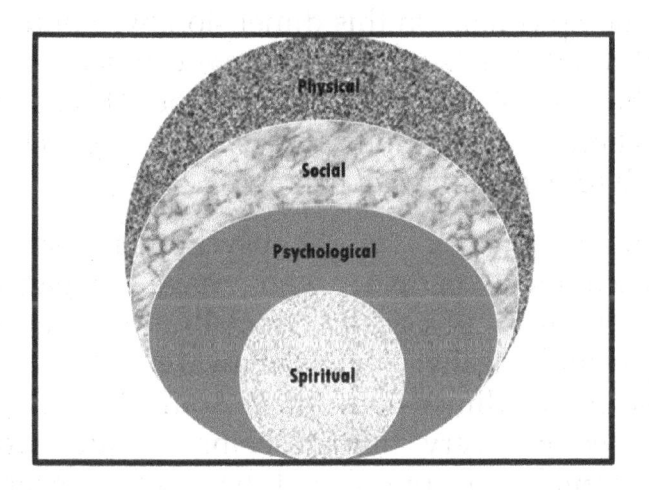

The Physical: On the physical dimension, we are *bodies interacting with the physical environment*. Our body is the point of contact with the world.

The Social: This is our interaction with the world of other people. Meaning is achieved through striving with others for the establishment of value, the most important commonly *shared value being 'Love'*

The Psychological: On the personal dimension, we connect through our 'self'. We are mainly pre-occupied with creating the very core of our being that gives us a *sense of stability, integration, and selfhood.* 'Meaning' on this level is created through a sense of self-worth, the knowledge that one is good and a valid person.

The Spiritual: On this dimension, we connect through our soul. This as we can see, is at the core of our being. This is the dimension wherein we find our *sense of belonging, value, identity, meaning and purpose.*

In my work as a psychotherapist, I encounter people who have engaged with life, physically, socially, and even psychologically, but unaware of their spiritual dimension, their soul. However, I see in every human being, a quest for meaning, for purpose. I have often heard my patients say, "Is this all there is to life, we are born, we are educated, we work, we marry, we procreate, and then grow old and die?" Isn't this why we need an awareness of our spiritual dimension, wherein we derive meaning and purpose? A meaningless life can feel empty and vain.

Existence – at the Core of Our 'Inner Being'

At the heart of the earth is a solid inner core made mainly of iron. But this inner core is layered by the outer core, the mantle and the crust. Just as God created the earth with an inner core made up of iron, He created in us, an inner core, which is our soul, as robust and substantial as iron. Just as it is necessary to get past the outer layers to reach the inner core, it is necessary to reach deep into our 'core-self' to access our spiritual dimension. *(My frame was not hidden from you when I was made in the secret place when I was woven together in the depths of the earth.* Psalm 139:15)

The word 'inner' means something within, insulated or layered by something outside, as in a covering. *(Though our outer man is decaying, yet our inner man is being renewed day by day.* 2 Corinthians 4:16) The meaning of the word 'being' is substance or existence. Every human being therefore is an existence of something substantial and meaningful.

The Hebrew translation for 'inner-being' is 'nephesh' which means, 'that which breathes', the 'breathing substance or being', the soul, the inner being. This explains that one's inner being really, is the soul. According to existential philosophers, the soul is the centre or seat of spirituality. The soul or the mind is the seat of thoughts and purposes.

The Story of Creation

The Bible records that (*before God, created the heavens and the earth, the earth was formless and empty, darkness was over the surface of the deep, and the spirit of God, hovered over the waters.* Genesis 1:1). This draws attention to the *'spirit'* of God that existed before 'existence' began. God created existence in the right order. He created the Universe in all its magnificence, and then, every living being upon the face of the earth. Finally, (*God created mankind, in his own image, male and female, he created them.* Genesis 1:27)

So, what really is this *'spirit'*? The word "spirit" comes from the Latin word *'spiritus'* and is related to the verb *'spirare'* which means "to breathe." In Genesis 2:7, we read, (*And the Lord God formed man of the dust of the ground and breathed into his nostrils the breath of life, and man became a living soul'*). In other words, God breathed His spirit into us. Thus, it is His *breath*, His *spirit* that constitutes our *soul*.

Every single one of us, therefore, is handcrafted by God the creator. This is what makes us living beings, distinct from animals and other species. Job explained this when he said (*The Spirit of God has made me, and the breath of the Almighty gives me life.* Job 33:4)

It is this 'spirit' at the core of our being that makes 'spirituality' a core dimension of our existence. Without this 'spirit' at the core, we will not be whole and complete. Philosophy called it the 'spiritual dimension' long before psychology became a separate academic discipline. (*I pray that you will be strengthened with power by His spirit in the inner man.* Ephesians 3:16)

The word 'psychology' comes from the Greek word 'psyche' which means soul, spirit, mind, life, and breath. Thus, the study of one's mental well-being really, is the study of one's inner being, the study of one's soul, the deepest self, or the essence of one's being. (Neil M Goldsmith; Psychology: the study of the Soul, 2010)

This explains that the soul of a human being came into existence through the breath of God. Without a soul, we would not have a conscious awareness of the need for love, a sense of belonging, acceptance, values, meaning and purpose. These are inherent within each of us. This is what we derive from the spiritual dimension. As this spiritual dimension is insulated deep inside of us, it takes diligent effort to tap into this inner core.

The human spirit is contained within an earthen vessel, our flesh, which is prone to making poor choices, failure, self-doubt, self-condemnation, guilt, shame, anger, anxiety, etc. Therefore, our spiritual dimension, our soul, needs to be nourished, nurtured, and replenished every day, or else it can become malnourished. Nurturing the soul is not a complex task, all it needs is love, the love of God, our Creator in our hearts, our love for self and for one another.

So, the question, 'who am I', really, is about my identity and the question 'why I am here on this earth', and 'why should I suffer', is about the meaning and purpose of life.

The Purpose of Life

Every one of us human beings knows that life is not devoid of suffering because we all have suffered in some ways, some more than others. Often, we are inclined to believe that our suffering is meaningless. But this may be because we lack the insight to perceive that meaning is derived, not automatic.

The moment I heard that my mother was no longer with us, it felt like I had just lost the meaning of my life. She was the one who gave me life, she was the one who gave me a reason to live. She was a large part of my very purpose and now that she was gone, I had no purpose left. The suffering I endured, watching her suffer, physically and emotionally, seemed to have culminated in total loss. What was the point in any of the suffering, hers, or mine?

My mother's suffering ended at the very moment she took her last breath. I am delighted for her but as for me, I needed to seek the meaning of my suffering. I did not have to look for long because just as I was catching the last glimpse of my mother's human body, going back into the dust of the earth, where it came from, and I was feeling desolate and alone, I sensed light entering my soul that had just been torn apart. That light was my discovery that through her suffering and death, my mother could continue to offer something precious if I was willing to pick up her legacy of love and carry it. I choose to reinvest my energy to engage more fully with my life to find meaning in my loss. Being alive is not about what we take from the world; it is all about what we give instead.

One of my friends who had only known my mother for just a few years said:

While others worked for earthly material gain that will perish, my aunty, Jessy was busy developing the minds and fashioning characters of her own children and many other daughters like me, modelling faith and character. Even when she was stressed beyond exhaustion, she used her love and faith to subdue negativity and find the strength to do what she needed to do, for her family. Her kindness is contagious, her memories awaken my faith and give me hope and positivity. Renuga Thilagaraj

> **Love is the reason for grief.**

Despite her absence, my mother's love gives me meaning, but first I need to grieve …

8. Grief at its Best...

The most beautiful people we have known are those that have known suffering, struggle, loss, and grief and have found their way out of the depths. These persons have an appreciation, a sensitivity and an understanding of life that fills them with compassion, gentleness, and a deep loving concern. Beautiful people do not just happen

Elizabeth Kubler-Ross

I must have been about five years of age, not long since starting school. My mother had just dropped me off and was leaving my classroom. I remember telling a child near me, "Look, that's my mother. Don't you think she is beautiful?". I honestly could not tell you what prompted me to make that comment. To an adult in the room, that must have been a silly little statement. In my eyes, as her child, she was the most beautiful woman on earth. But the way I saw her over the years, never changed. She still is the most beautiful person I know. Her simplicity and humility positioned her to understand others' pain with compassion and kindness despite her own struggles and pain. Her beauty is an incorruptible one.

A large part of her suffering was caused by her own grief and loss. The loss of her beloved mother, her father, her older sister, and her older brothers crushed her heart. She did not express her grief as much as she would have wanted to, because her responsibilities as a wife and mother took over her life and she would always put others' needs first. When I did speak to her about her loss, I could see the pain etched on her face, at the memory of the beloved ones she lost. But she would always say to me that even though she was in sorrow over their loss, she was happy they were safe home, no longer in pain. My mother never shared her sorrow with me or the others in the family as she believed it was her responsibility to make her family and others around her happy. I could, of course, sense her pain although I never once heard or saw her cry. She somehow found her way out of the depths, with a greater appreciation and understanding of life. Her beauty did not just happen.

Grief Defined

The American Psychological Association (APA) defines 'grief' as the anguish experienced after a significant loss, usually the death of a beloved person. Grief often includes physiological distress, separation anxiety, confusion, yearning, obsessive dwelling on the past, and apprehension about the future. Intense grief can become life-threatening through disruption of the immune system, self-neglect, and suicidal thoughts. For some, grief may take the form of regret over something lost, remorse for something done or sorrow for a mishap to oneself.

Over the many years of my professional life, I have written about, talked about, and taught 'grief' but when my mother breathed her last, I was not thinking about how I should grieve. I could not sit down and analyse the theory of grief. I had inadvertently started to grieve. It felt automatic. I wailed, I wept, I cried, I talked aloud to my mother about how disappointed I was that she would leave, for good, without giving me a chance to say goodbye to her, thanking her for being my mother. When I was exhausted from crying, I fell asleep. This to me, was my process of grieving. I became deeply distressed, anxious about my separation from my mother, apprehensive about my future, the future of my dad, and regretful about the million things I could have done for her. However, whilst I could feel the pain of my loss washing over me,

I did not feel overwhelmed as I became aware that she left a beautiful legacy of tender compassionate love, a legacy I could pick up and carry forward.

Every day of my work life, grief enters my room and when it does, I embrace it, as that is the only way I can help my patients grieve. I have facilitated the process of grieving for many. Now, that I had to grieve my own loss, I felt lost, to begin with, but once I began to feel my pain and embrace it, I could look for the meaning in my grief.

Death is ...

Death is nothing at all.

I have only slipped into the next room.

I am I and you are you, and the old life that we lived so fondly together is untouched, unchanged.

Whatever we were to each other, that we are still.

Call me by my old familiar name. Speak to me in the way you always used to.

Put no difference in your tone. Wear no forced air of solemnity or sorrow.

Laugh as we always laughed at the little jokes we enjoyed together. Play, smile, think of me

Let my name be ever the household word that it always was. Let it be spoken without effect, without the ghost of a shadow upon it.

Life means all that it ever meant.

It is the same as it ever was.

There is absolute and unbroken continuity.

Why should I be out of mind because I am out of sight?

I am waiting for you, for an interval, somewhere very near, just around the corner.

All is well. Nothing is hurt; nothing is lost.

One brief moment and all will be as it was before.

How we shall laugh at the trouble of parting when we meet again
>
> – Henry Scott Holland

These were some of the most comforting words I had ever read in the time I grieved. I have learned, not to avoid the pain of my mother's absence, but to make her a part of my household conversations, to include her in my daily thought life. My thoughts of my mother are less painful because I can think fondly of the good and beautiful times we have had together. As I think of her, I can commune with her, in my spirit, and I am comforted.

Grief is not defined as the acute emotional pain or anguish of losing a loved one, it is our response to our loss, whichever way we choose to respond. While bereavement refers to the state of 'loss', grief is our reaction to that loss.

The Stages of Grief

Elizabeth Kubler-Ross (1926-2004), psychiatrist and pioneer of the death-and-dying movement, explained that people experiencing grief generally go through a series of emotions, shock and denial, anger, resentment and guilt, bargaining, depression, and acceptance. Most people experience these series of emotions, but not necessarily in a certain order. Grief is unique for every individual.

Up until her book 'Death and Dying' was published in 1969, death and dying was a socially forbidden subject. Today, death is not a prohibited subject, dying is not considered morbid but people avoid talking about a loved one that has died for fear that it will bring back painful memories. People seem to believe that talking about a loved one who has died will stir up painful emotions and that this will not lend to healing in any way.

On returning to the UK, I was glad to meet with some of my friends, who comforted me with thoughtful condolence messages. However, when I met them, they did not talk to me about my mother or the pain of my loss. We talked about everything else but my mother. I wondered if this was possibly because they wanted to protect me from being reminded about my loss. I thought that perhaps people felt, that talking about it would cause more distress or were afraid that they would not know how to cope if I were to cry. I knew that talking about my mother would only relieve my pain. But somehow people did not perceive it that way. Not talking about it caused me more pain. *"It is not what comes out of us, but what remains inside of us, that makes us sick. You cannot heal what you do not feel"* Dr Edith Egar

In my grief work with my patients, I always allow the time and space for narratives of their loss and any narratives of their loved ones. The bereaved are often tearful but it is the expression of the loss that releases the pain and brings about healing. Dr Egar reiterates, *"the opposite of depression is expression"*

Healthy Grieving

Stroebe and Schutt (1999) explained that bereaved people have been observed to either alternate between spending all their time dwelling on their loss or completely avoiding thinking about their loss, by keeping busy. This takes away the opportunity to process grief and such people are likely to experience long-term dysfunction.

Healthy grieving should be a *dual process*, of taking time to process grief on the one hand and engage with the daily responsibilities of life on the other. This will help experience a range of emotions, thereby helping find the balance between being restorative and loss orientated.

For the first twenty-four hours after I received news of my mother's death, I could not cry, could not really think, or speak coherently. I could not function. My body could not keep still. I did not force myself to do anything I could not do. I needed to accept my body's reaction. The next day, all I could do was cry. While I wailed, I released a lot of pain, pain that had been produced by the fear of losing my mother, particularly during the last few weeks I noticed my mother was rapidly going downhill. After I arrived at my parents' home for the funeral, it felt comforting to be with family and friends who had gathered in large numbers, to join us in bidding farewell to my beloved mother. Although I was with my dad and my sister's family in the two weeks following the funeral, I often withdrew into my own space, to allow my pain to surface so I could feel my pain, confront it, and process it. At other times, I shared my grief with my family, and this alleviated my distress.

I noticed that on returning home from India, I had the space I needed, to grieve, just the way I wanted to, but I realised that life was never going to be the same. I felt rudely awakened every morning to the new reality that my mother was no longer here in my world, that I would never ever be able to see her or hear her voice. Without any warning or preparation, my lifeworld had changed. Strangely enough, I found myself sleeping most of the days and nights.

It felt like my body was weary with the pain I had carried for some time, it was not just the pain of having lost my mother but also the anxiety of what the future would hold for me, without my mother. Up until this point in my life, I had not fully appreciated just how much I depended on my mother's love, for my mental and emotional well-being.

After two weeks of excessive sleeping, I began to re-establish my work routine. I recognised my grief felt less heavy as I worked my way through the first few weeks, part working, and part grieving. This is the dual-process model of grieving I experienced, oscillating between dwelling on my loss and going about my usual work. This felt like a healthy balance.

Grief Serves a Purpose

Grief serves a purpose. When I first felt a strange numbness, my body was shutting down so that the reality of my loss could be integrated slowly, it was a healthy reaction as I was emotionally ill-prepared to handle the loss of my mother with no notice. A few days later, I was beginning to feel depressed. But depression allowed me to withdraw from external stimulation for a while, to turn inwards and reflect on what had just happened. This is the time I slept. While my body needed to rest and sleep, my mind was relaxing, allowing my emotions to surface. It would be very dangerous to not allow these painful emotions to be expressed, as they would manifest in unhealthy patterns of thinking and behaving. For example, unexpressed grief or stifled grief could manifest as anger. Thus, depression or a withdrawal of self from the world would allow for a reflection within, taking one into a deeper place of being, giving oneself permission to feel the emotions of disappointment, sorrow, and emptiness.

This is the process that is moving me from a place of utter meaninglessness to a place of acceptance, strength, and the courage to engage fully with life.

It is nearly three months now, since my mother passed away and I can confidently say that as I allow my pain to be confronted and experienced, I embrace my loss and as I embrace my loss, I re-engage with my life, I move forward.

> **When grief is not attended to, or processed, it fills the heart with emptiness. The only way to process grief is to grieve. Processing grief can empower 'self' to re-engage with life with fresh meaning and purpose.**

A Continuing Bond

About a month after my loss, I found myself crying one day and was asked the question, "I thought by now, you would have got over it". At this point, I realised it was going to be difficult for me to openly allow an expression of my pain. It felt like I no longer had permission to grieve unless I did it in the privacy of my own space. Being expected to overcome grief within a given time frame or being expected to emotionally disengage with my mother, did not facilitate my continued engagement and participation in life, in my world.

Grief does not have a timeline nor is there a set time frame to allow, for people to grieve. It is not linear. Every one of us will grieve differently, not necessarily in the same order of the stages, or within a certain time frame, but grieve, we must.

The pain of my loss will never go away, this is my 'continuing bond' as Tonkins (1996) described. The loss that stays inside of us, really is the bond staying in, while I continue to engage with life. This is really, what empowers me to continue to interact with my 'self' and the world, in more meaningful ways, finding new strength, a deeper understanding, and better esteem of self.

Grief sometimes washes over me like a wave, and I realise I need to release my pain. If I don't, I could lock it in and that is unhealthy. If tears are my way of doing this, can I allow myself to cry? When is it appropriate to cry?

9. Tears: Is it ok to Cry?

Tears, the silent language of grief, are God's gift to us (Voltaire). It is our holy water that heals us while they flow. (Rita Schiano)

Processing grief is a unique experience which is why different people grieve differently. For one it may be endless talking about the beloved one they lost, for another, it could be crying and wailing, for another, quietly retreating to reflect on their loss. For some, it may just be a more intense engagement with their work, to keep busy, or even aiming to achieve more by way of setting off their pain. For many people, it will be a combination of everything in different stages perhaps. Whatever the response, the bereaved will grieve, whether consciously or not.

In the first few hours of receiving the news of my mother's passing, I could not talk, could not cry, could not move. My initial reaction of 'denial' served as an emotional anaesthesia, so I would not be overwhelmed by my loss. I was not in denial of my loss. I was in denial of my need to express my grief. This is the body's natural defence mechanism. But shortly after, it became a matter of tears. For the first few weeks, I spent a lot of time crying and found that that was my only way of expressing my grief. My tears were my only comfort. I could not, not cry.

Time and time again, I hear these words in a session with most of my patients, "I am so sorry, to be crying" "please excuse my tears", and "sorry I did not mean to cry". I have had to assure my patients, that it's good to cry because tears are a healthy way to release pain. I have always encouraged my patients to cry. Shedding tears is not the only way people grieve, however, those who need to cry, seem to seek approval because society has conditioned us to believe that 'tears' are offensive in public as they can cause emotional discomfort.

No Need to Cry

To my surprise, many people told me to stop crying when I began to cry. At first, I was told, I should not wail as my mother's spirit would be disturbed. I know that the spirit of a departed soul is alive and that angels accompany the spirit of the departed one, into the presence of our Creator. (*Angels carried Lazarus to Abraham's Bosom, which was also called Paradise by Jesus.* Luke 23:43).

I also know that our loving God who called my mother home, will not deny me the need to feel my pain and express it. (*Blessed are those who mourn, for they shall be comforted.* Mathew 5:4).

Then, at the funeral, many well-intentioned people told me there was no need to cry as my mother was after all in a much better place. She was indeed, but I was not. I had just lost the most precious human connection in my life, and I was devastated. All I was doing was expressing my pain. I needed to walk the journey of my grief, and this journey is a process. For many of us, tears facilitate the process of grief.

The Stigma of Tears

I remember, years ago, I was visiting my uncle whose wife had passed away a year prior to my visit. I asked if I could see the photos of the funeral. As I looked at the photos, I started to weep as I was very close to my aunt, and I felt extremely sad about my loss. I noticed as I wept that no one else appeared to be tearful or sad, as I was. I knew that they had already walked their journey of grief for a whole year and were in a different place than where I was. I was aware that I cannot be judgmental of how people should grieve or when. We each adapt different ways of grieving, at different paces. But somehow, I was hoping that someone would enter my space of grief although it was my need to grieve, not theirs, as they had started their process of grieving a year ago. It seemed as if I was all by myself in my grief. Perhaps they did not want to stir up feelings of their own grief that they had buried. While I wanted to grieve the loss of my beloved aunt, I wanted to share in their grief too. I am not quite sure why, but suddenly it felt like it was inappropriate to cry. It was almost as if 'crying' was forbidden.

On another occasion, I was visiting the family of one of my aunts that had passed away. It was about a couple of years since my aunt had passed away. Just as I was leaving, I mentioned just how much I missed my aunty. I did not envisage any kind of resistance to this comment because I knew everyone was missing her. However, the response was 'silence', which I interpreted as 'please let's not talk about her, it will upset everyone'. I could well understand that they were all trying to protect one another from bringing up the pain, so I left quietly, but with a sad and heavy heart, sad because we could not share the pain of our loss, heavy because I restrained myself from telling them that it was far better to talk about the pain of our loss and shed tears if we have to, than to silently carry our sorrow alone. I recognised then that, being restrained from expressing my pain and suppressing my tears heightened my anguish of grief.

The Truth Behind Tears

Dr William Frey, a biochemist, and tear expert, explained that *"emotional tears contain stress hormones that get excreted from the body through crying. Tears shed toxins that accumulate during stress. Crying stimulates the production of endorphins, our body's natural pain killer and feel-good hormones"*. From my own experience now, I know that crying releases pain and produces a feeling of comfort and calm within.

What Happens if We Don't Cry?

"Crying is essentially a release valve that rids our body of excess stress and tension. When we hold back our tears, our brain signals our adrenal glands to release stress hormones such as adrenaline and cortisol. These chemicals boost heart rate and blood pressure which can translate into chest tightness and sometimes palpitation, messing with appetite and blood sugar levels". - Dr Nicole Van Groningen

Most people do want to cry but some do not feel the need to cry. Research suggests that those who feel the need to cry, should not suppress their tears. Stifled tears are stifled emotions, and this causes physical and emotional stress. Often, suppressed stress and tension can cause angry outbursts. I have sometimes observed people lashing out unreasonably and later discover that there has either been a death in their family or that they have unaddressed trauma in their life. These are people who are embarrassed to acknowledge the pain of their loss, afraid to allow themselves to feel vulnerable, and afraid to shed their tears for fear of distressing others around them. So, they deny themselves an expression of their grief, like I have done, sometimes. Grief then translates into anger and becomes detrimental to their relationships, more importantly, to their mental wellbeing.

The Gift of Tears

Tears are God's gift to us because they are the language of grief when grief has no words. As the tears flow, so does the pain, out of the body, washing away the stress, and calming the nervous system. Tears remove the toxic substances from our bodies and help us accept our loss with courage, strength, and dignity.

After the first few hours of total shock and numbness, I started to cry as my tears flooded my being. I cried inconsolably throughout the first two days. On arriving beside my mother's lifeless body, I cried incessantly. My tears were persistent. However, I felt comforted by my tears. It did not feel as persistent a few days after the funeral and slowly over the weeks and months, my tears have become fewer.

As I write this now, it is about four months since losing my mother. I still cry but this is now a rare occasion. The tears I shed immediately after my loss, have greatly helped me to express my pain and I can feel my nervous system is calmer now than it was when I was first confronted by the news of my loss.

Historically, we seem to have been conditioned into believing that tears are a sign of weakness and vulnerability. 'It is not right to cry in public', 'Men don't cry'. But *"tears really are a sign of courage, strength, and authenticity"* -Dr Judith Orloff. I can resonate with this because personally, I know it has taken me courage to be authentic with my true self of feeling devastated when I did. I know I was brave, to expose my sadness, my vulnerability. Crying as I did over the last few months has made me feel emotionally stronger now. I no longer feel fragmented and fragile like I did, at the start of my grieving process.

For me, my tears have been an integral part of my grieving and have helped me express and heal my pain. Nothing, however, can alter the abrupt absolute end of life. The permanence of death can feel intimidating.

> **Denying tears does not dissolve emotional pain, it solidifies it**
>
> **Allowing tears releases and heals pain**

Death is the permanent cessation of the functions of the human body, but is it the end of existence?

10. Is Death the End of Existence?

> No single atom in creation can go out of existence; it only changes in form. No energy or force is ever destroyed; it is only changed from one form to another
>
> Burris Jenkins

It seems that while my mother was alive, she loved and gave of herself, not just to those that loved her, but to everyone that she encountered in her life. 'Being alive' for my mother, meant 'giving'. It was in her 'giving' that she found meaning and purpose. If she was not giving someone a cup of cold water or a cup of tea or a hot plate of food, or even money or clothes, she was giving a listening ear to understand, her compassion, her warmth, and affection, her forgiveness of those that offended and hurt her. She did not differentiate, nor played favouritism. She gave and gave of herself until the very last breath of her life. To my mother, existence meant, 'to give'. But her giving does not seem to have ended with her last breath.

Defining Existence

The word 'existence' denotes a state of 'being' in the world. The term 'existence' is derived from the Latin word 'existere' which means to 'come forth', to 'be manifest', to 'emerge', 'be visible', 'to come to light', 'to stand forth', 'to be produced'. From an existential philosophical perspective, the focus of existence has been 'what it means to be alive'.

The impact that my mother's unconditional sacrificial love made on me and the others that knew her is now being made manifest, it is emerging. As I think, reflect, recount, and write about my mother's life, the real core of her 'being' is becoming visible, coming to light. Through her death, my mother has taught me, what it means to be alive. Since the 'spirit' does not die, we can see that her spirit of kindness, compassion and forgiveness, is alive. In essence, my mother exists. She has moved on from the earthly realm into the heavenly realm. Her 'being' is now that of a different state and in that she exists, no longer as an earthly human being, but as a heavenly being, in the very presence of her creator. In effect, she is still a 'being', a human 'being' no longer, but a spiritual 'being'. This is not incomprehensible as the meaning of the word 'being' is 'existence'.

'Death' in the Context of Human Existence

The components that collectively define human existence are the body, the mind, the soul, and the spirit. In other words, the dimensions of human existence are physical, social, psychological, and spiritual. So, existence really is not all about life in one's human body. What is central to existence is the 'spirit' in the 'spiritual realm'.

'Death' is medically defined as the cessation of all the vital functions of an organism which is the human body. This draws attention to the reality that the spirit and the soul are not part of death. It can be concluded then that if human existence is a collective function of the body, mind, soul, and spirit; and death is the cessation of the body, then the spirit is indestructible.

Death cannot be the end of existence as existence does not just refer to the body. The body is only the physical dimension of existence. The mind, in other words, is the psychological dimension and the spirit, the spiritual dimension. This posits that the spirit and soul of a human being are incorruptible.

When Jesus stepped out alive from the tomb where he was buried, He demonstrated the irreversible truth that our physical bodies will one day cease to function, but our souls will enter the presence of the Living God. (*For God so loved the world, that he gave his only Son, that whoever believes in him should not perish but have eternal life.* John 3:16)

'Spirit' in the Spiritual Dimension

The 'Spirit' is the non-physical part of a person which is the seat of emotions and character, the soul, according to the oxford dictionary.

The Hebrew word 'ruach' is the origin of the word spirit which is the breath of Yahweh which carries His life force. The *Greek* origin for the word 'spirit' is 'pneuma' which means 'breath'. In ancient Greek medicine, the word 'pneuma' was used to indicate the form of circulating air necessary for the systemic functioning of vital organs. It is the material that sustains consciousness in a body. The 'spirit' then, really is the life force of every human being.

Since God is the life-giver, the life-breath comes from Him, and man lives as long as God's breath remains in him (Isaiah 42:5b). *When God withdraws His breath, the flesh returns to the dust of the earth, the ground* (Psalm 146:4); *and the spirit returns to God who gave it* (Ecclesiastes 12:7). This affirms that the spirit is indestructible while the body perishes. The body perishes when the spirit leaves the body because there is no longer 'breath' circulating the air necessary for the systemic functioning of vital organs. There is no more consciousness.

Existence Cannot be Annihilated

The first law of 'thermodynamics' states that neither energy (which is our soul and spirit) nor matter (as in our body) can be destroyed. They can be transformed but never annihilated, in other words, they can never be reduced to non-existence.

"Jesus Christ gave us proof of immortality, and yet it would hardly seem necessary that one should rise from the dead to convince us that the grave is not the end. If the Father stoops to touch with divine power the cold and pulseless heart of the buried acorn and to make it burst forth into a new life, will He leave neglected in the earth the soul of man, made in the image of his Creator? If He stoops to give to the rosebud whose withered blossoms float upon the autumn breeze, the sweet assurance of another springtime, will He refuse... words of hope to the sons of men when the frosts of winter come? I am as sure that there is another life as I am that I live today!" - William J Bryan

Since my mother passed away, my heart searches for her, yearns for her presence, her look of love, her tender touch of compassion, and her gentle voice. In the physical realm, for me, it is a matter of absence, but spiritually speaking, I know that her soul has burst into new life. Her spirit and her life force have changed forms. This means that while she is physically absent in her body, here on earth, she is present in her spirit, with our Lord. (*We are confident, yes, well pleased rather to be absent from the body and to be present with the Lord.* 2 Corinthians 5:8). Just as I carry her spirit in mine, all those who knew her as a friend, a sister, and a mother, carry in their spirit, a part of what she imparted through her gentle tender compassionate love.

Death, the Birth of a New Beginning

Death is not the end of existence. It is the end of an era, one which marks a new beginning. The existence of my mother has now begun in the spirit realm, of heaven itself. This has been documented in John 11: 25-26 (*Jesus said to her, "I am the resurrection and the life. The one who believes in me will live, even though they die; and whoever lives by believing in me will never die"*).

It was about two years ago, at the very beginning of the pandemic, when 'going on walks' was the most exciting event of my day, and I was walking one morning,

Is Death the End of Existence? | 97

I stopped unexpectedly as I could smell something very sweet and wondered what it was. I soon realised it was the smell of a flower, I thought, 'well that smells familiar but a fragrance I had not experienced in a very long time'. At this point I felt compelled to look for the source of that sweet scent. I quickly discovered I was walking past someone's front garden that had a jasmine plant. The jasmine flower was in full bloom, and it was the scent of this jasmine that had stopped me in my tracks! Here in the UK, the jasmine plant is not common to find, which is why I was surprised. I stopped and I thought, 'there is something distinct about a jasmine'. Like any other flower it smells sweet, but the scent of a jasmine penetrates one's soul. It is a naturally far-reaching fragrance. Such is the fragrance of the sacrificial love of my mother Jasmine. It has reached near and far, many a broken heart. Hers' is a fragrance that will never die, an existence that will never cease.

In the Old Testament of the bible, the blood of an animal had to be sacrificially poured out as an atonement for sin. But in the New Testament, Jesus poured out His blood as an atonement for our sins. So, we do not have to slaughter animals for our sins now. Jesus did this willingly because He loved us. His life became the fragrant offering, a sweet-smelling savour. Just as the fragrance of His sacrificial love will never die, the blood Jesus shed on the cross will never lose its power.

As a daughter, a sister, a wife, a mother and a friend, my mother poured out her life unselfishly, loved without expecting anything in return. Her heart was always full of compassion and empathy even towards people who did not deserve it, like those who offended and oppressed her. She would willingly sacrifice anything for anyone, not just those close to her. The sweet-smelling savour of her sacrifice, the fragrance of her love cannot lose its power.

My mother (extreme left) with her parents, brothers and sisters

**May our sons in their youth be like plants full grown,
And our daughters like corner pillars fashioned for a palace.**

Psalm 144:12

During her lifetime, my mother walked in love. Her love was an unselfish one in that she always had others' best interests at heart because she valued every individual for who they were, just as we read in Ephesians 5:1-2 (*Follow Christ's example and value one another – practice empathy and compassion, unselfishly seeking the best for others, just as Christ also loved you and gave Himself up as an offering and sacrifice to God, a sweet fragrance*).

My mother's life here on earth has ended, but the fragrance of her unselfish, unconditional love that has penetrated deep into the souls of those that knew her, is now giving birth to the new beginning of meaning and purpose. It is through this 'meaning' that her lingering fragrance will touch the lives of people she did not know.

Death is not the end of existence, but the death of a loved one heightens our awareness of the brevity of life here on this earth. Since life here on this earth is finite, it is of paramount importance that we walk in conscious awareness of who we are as God's creation. It's when we know ourselves, that we can know and understand others, love deeply enough to understand the true essence of another and bring out the best in them. This is what my mother always did.

She took time to bring out the best in me and in everyone that knew her. She cared enough to do this because she loved deeply enough.

Make Time to Stop and Smell the Roses

I vividly remember my mother's sixtieth birthday. I was visiting my parents and I had the pleasure of celebrating her big birthday with my young son. On the evening of her birthday, we decided to go for a prayer meeting, followed by dinner. At this meeting, I went up on stage, informed people it was my mother's birthday, and told them about how precious my mother's life and love was, because it was a love poured out of her sacrifice. I thanked God for her life and in the presence of all the people there, wished her happy birthday. She was of course displeased with me as I had publicly applauded her. She never wanted publicity of any kind because she always believed she was not worthy of praise. I told everyone at that meeting, that my mother was the most valuable person in my life and that I was not going to wait for her to be gone, to drop my roses on her grave. I wanted to give her as many roses as I possibly could, while she was with us. I am so glad I did.

Scientific research demonstrates that stopping to smell roses, enhances cognitive function. The fragrance of roses gives the human brain a learning boost which allows retention of learned knowledge and skills and has been proved to result in significant success amongst students.

If the physical act of smelling a rose can change one's cognitive function, how much more can an act of appreciation and validation, impact one's emotional and mental well-being? Validation is simply making room for another's feelings and allowing them to feel their feelings without trying to fix them. Just as the scent of a rose can enhance the cognitive function, the act of appreciation and validation can enhance one's sense of self, making one feel valued and worthwhile, loved, and accepted.

If one word of appreciation and validation, one smile of approval and affirmation, or one look of understanding can help change someone's view of self, cause them to perceive their world differently, enhancing their mental resilience to keep living, keep giving and keep moving, and enjoy the God-given meaning and purpose of their life, then could we not all spread the same fragrance, just as my mother did.

Jasmine

Your fragrance lingers

Epilogue

About 18 years ago, God impressed upon my heart to write a book. He gave me the title and I wrote this down in my prayer journal. But I had just given birth to my child and did not believe I could make the time then, to initiate the process of writing a book. I asked God to wait until my baby grew up. My baby did grow up, went to school, and has even flown the nest now. But I had completely forgotten about the book God asked me to write. However, the day my mother was buried, became the day I was propelled into obeying God to start writing.

But then, I had never written a book before and so did not know where or how to begin, until I happened to re-connect with a friend, I had met twenty-four years ago in a training workshop, through a common friend Sowmya. From the time I mentioned the book, he, Dr Arun Viswanath, began to encourage me to get started. I honestly did not think it would be feasible for me to write this, given my work schedule and lack of experience, but because of the consistent and gentle encouragement from both Sowmya and Arun, I hesitantly started to write. Arun amid his busy work life and travel, took time to read every single chapter that I wrote and spent a few minutes talking to me about it, one at a time, critically evaluating my writing, giving me a variety of ideas, thus enabling me to bring out my best into my writing. Sowmya, on the other hand consistently encouraged me, read my manuscript and offered her critical evaluation, which helped me reflect on my work, from a different perspective.

God will turn the Universe, if He must, to bring the right people beside us, to help us accomplish the purpose of our life. Having read through my book, Arun wistfully said: "I'm sorry, I did not have the chance to meet this remarkable extraordinary lady of grace" Indeed, she was the most gracious woman I have ever known all my life. I write about her, so that she will continue to inspire those she did not have a chance to meet.

When I started to write, I had no structure in my mind, no idea of what exactly should go into this book. As I wrote down the title and sat still, the spirit of God began to impress His thoughts on my heart, to be presented in this book. It was God who gave me the title of the book and the title of each chapter. So,

Epilogue | 107

if you have arrived at the end of this book and are not the same as you were when you started reading it, then it means you have been touched by my mother's life and her love, you have been moved by the spirit of God, our Creator.

Writing this book has been a grieving journey for me. Many a time, I had to stop writing, just to allow space for my tears. But those tears have healed and transformed me in ways I could not describe. I am not the same person I was when I started writing this, she (my mother) as always, has touched me and healed me of my sorrow. My tears have been the expression of my pain of losing my mother but reflecting on the love that I have received from my mother all through my life and listening to others' accounts of what my mother meant to them, has filled my heart with a new motivation to fulfil my God-given purpose. Just as my life will never be the same again, I hope you too are inspired by the story of my mother's sacrificial love and that it will propel you into using your God-given potential for the glory of His Kingdom.

I know this book may be just a drop in the ocean but isn't one drop enough to create ripples. As Andy Andrews put it, *"You have been created to make a difference. You have within you, the power to change the world"*. Changing the world can begin with just one ...

> **One gesture of love, one act of kindness, one word that will validate, one loving smile, one look of compassion is all it will take, to wipe away the hopelessness and despair in someone's heart and through one heart, many others.**